EMERSON ON
SOUND MONEY

By

WILLIS GEORGE EMERSON

First published in 1896

British Library Cataloguing-in-Publication Data
A catalogue record for this book is available
from the British Library

CONTENTS

Willis George Emerson................................5

SPEECH OF HON. WILLIS GEORGE EMERSON, ...7

KNOWS "COIN" HARVEY. 8

THE PEOPLE A JURY................................8

MORAL QUESTIONS INVOLVED.....................9

WILSON LAW CLOSED FACTORIES. 11

BREAD AND BUTTER THE ISSUE. 12

JACKSON AND JEFFERSON. 13

GREENBACKS WERE CHEAP MONEY. 14

HONESTY AND SOBER JUDGMENT NEEDED.......17

PER CAPITA OF MONEY. 18

I AM A BIMETALLIST...............................18

THE CRIME OF '73................................20

CONSISTENT FRIEND OF SILVER. 21

DO NOT DEMAND BIMETALLISM. 22

FREE TRADE SHOULD BE UNDONE..................23

GOES AFTER BRYAN. 24

IMPROVED HARVESTING METHODS...............25

WHY ARE THEY NOT HONEST?....................26

SHALL PRICES BE RESTORED......................27

PROTECTIVE TARIFF THE REMEDY. 28

THE QUESTION IS SIMPLY ONE OF HONESTY
OR DISHONESTY. 28

LABORERS SHALL BE HONESTLY REWARDED. 29

A PRINCIPLE UPHELD BY STATESMEN.. 30

ENGLAND HAS BEEN SERVED. 31

HE TALKS OF WOOL.. 32

WHAT THE RECORD IS.. 33

SPIRIT OF REVOLUTION.. 34

REAT IS CONFIDENCE.. 35

PROUD OF BEING A REPUBLICAN. 37

MARCHING TO GREATEST VICTORY. 38

WILLIS GEORGE EMERSON

Willis George Emerson was born in 1856, and spent his early education at Knox College, Illinois, USA. He later attended *Northern Ohio University*, after which he was admitted to the bar in 1886. Emerson quickly lost interest in the legal profession however, and moved to Kansas where he became heavily involved in politics; actively campaigning on behalf of the Republican Party in both the 1888 and 1900 elections. Emerson is best known as a prominent American novelist though, and is famed for his evocative tales of the Mid-West. Among his better-known novels are *Buell Hampton* (1902), *The Builders* (1906), *Smoky God vs. Voyage in the Inner World* (1908), *The Treasure of Hidden Valley* (1915) and *The Man Who Discovered Himself* (1919). *Smoky God vs. Voyage in the Inner World* is particularly notable for its unusual plotline; the protagonist discovers an Eden like civilisation in in the centre of the earth, where a scientifically advanced race of long-lived giants is discovered worshipping a 'smoky God' – the interior sun. This was the first literary work to bring Emerson widespread acclaim. A man of many talents and interests, Emerson also worked as a newspaperman, lawyer, politician and promoter, forming the North American Copper Company in Wyoming. Emerson is also credited with founding the town of Grand Encampment, a municipality in Carbon County, Wyoming. With Emerson's Copper Company based there, it became a booming centre of copper mining and smelting. A sixteen-mile tramway was built to carry copper ore from the mountains into the town for smelting; a tramway which was, at the time, the longest in the world. He died on 11 December, 1918.

SPEECH OF HON. WILLIS GEORGE EMERSON,

LOCKERBY HALL, GRAND RAPIDS, MICHIGAN.
OCTOBER 29, 1896.

Mr. Chairman, Ladies and Gentlemen—I am indeed pleased to meet such a magnificent audience in this manufacturing city of Grand Rapids, noted from ocean to ocean for her culture, commerce and progress. Especially am I pleased to speak in your city in behalf of sound money, protection and reciprocity, under the auspices of the Young Men's Republican Club. I bring you greeting from the state of Illinois, and promise you that she will give a majority of 150,000 on next Tuesday for William McKinley. I am proud to hail from the grand old state of Illinois—a state that gave to our common country in the darkest days of our nation's history, Logan, that matchless civilian general; gave the unconquerable Grant, the tanner from Galena, and offered up as a holy sacrifice the "rail-splitter" president from the Sangamon bottoms—Abraham Lincoln. But to-night I remember that I am in the state of Michigan—magnificent commonwealth—almost illimitable in her resources, unconquerable in her courage, phenomenal in her progress, invincible in her pluck, unswerving in her patriotism, the home of the gallant Alger, and the former abode of that matchless statesman and patriot—the gifted Zach Chandler. Fellow citizens, we are in the closing days of the most momentous political campaign ever witnessed in our common country. He who would question the sincerity or honesty of a political opponent's views in this crusade must for the time being forget the school house on the hill and the high plain of intelligence of American citizenship.

KNOWS "COIN" HARVEY.

Hon. W. H. Harvey, author of Coin's Financial School, is a gentleman I have known for many years, and for as many years as we have known each other, we have been warm personal friends. Toward the man I entertain the greatest respect; toward his theories I regard them as idle, visionary sophistries as unstable as "the house that was built upon sand." The student who really gives thought to the financial question will early discover that Coin's Financial School rests upon a false foundation and the superstructure must surely fall when beat against by the irresistable and truth capped waves of facts and history. No better answer can be given to these misleading and false theories than a plain, truthful statement of our coinage laws and the effect of legislation relating thereto. Fellow citizens, whatever else we may be, we are all Americans, either by birth or adoption; we respect and love the same flag and the undying principles which it represents. We do not differ in a desire for good government. We may differ and differ widely, however, in our opinions and ideas as to what laws will insure the greatest blessings to the people of this nation. Fortunately for the Republican party the American people are a reading and a thinking people, and the problems of the present campaign are now on trial before a jury of 70,000,000 of honest peers, not one of whom am I willing to believe would wantonly strike down the flag of our country, or any of its cherished institutions.

THE PEOPLE A JURY.

This audience is a part of that great jury, who, after the evidence is all in, will decide one way or the other, with an avalanche of snowy ballots, as spotless in their purity as the honest hearts of the voters who cast the verdict into the ballot boxes. As Americans we are justly proud of our birthright—

proud of the air of freedom that kisses the stars and stripes—our nation's ensign, emblematical of mighty victories in the past, a guarantee of protection in the present to all who stand beneath its folds and laden with rich promises of future prosperity. Our country is greater than the men whose election it is our pleasure to advocate. It is not men but measures which we are to consider. An earnest conscientious desire to investigate and determine the right, should absorb and thrill the heart of every patriotic American voter. The great parties in the present campaign do not differ so much in regard to the amount of money as they do in regard to its quality. "It is not the medium of exchange so much as it is an active exchange of the medium itself." On the tariff question we do not differ in schedules, but principles— principles which we, as republicans believe, involve the welfare of all our people and the prosperity of all classes. Personally I have every respect for a conscientious, earnest opponent in this crusade of education, and while honestly differing from them, yet will endeavor to wound the feelings of none. If I speak bitterly of doctrines which I believe to be pernicious in theory and ruinous in practice, do me the justice of not interpreting my remarks as in any sense personal.

MORAL QUESTIONS INVOLVED.

Fellow citizens, this is a campaign embracing both political and moral questions. It is a political conflict, which the people will sooner or later acknowledge, to be one of patriotism. A moral conflict, which they will acknowledge to be indeed sublime.

WE MUST NOT FORGET THAT PATRIOTISM IN TIME OF PEACE IS A SCARCER ARTICLE THAN IN TIMES OF WAR.

In the guise of citizens men like "Coin" Harvey are attempting ignorantly or otherwise to undermine and overthrow our nation's honor and credit, and it is these alone that can perpetuate our liberties and insure us prosperity.

THE REPUBLICAN PARTY COMES BEFORE
THE AMERICAN PEOPLE ADVOCATING THE
MAINTENANCE OF THE GOLD STANDARD AND
THE USE OF SILVER AS MONEY, IN THE LARGEST
VOLUME POSSIBLE, CONSISTENT WITH SAFETY;
ADVOCATING THE MAINTENANCE OF OUR
NATION'S HONOR AND CREDIT; ADVOCATING
A TARIFF, NOT FOR REVENUE ONLY, BUT A
PROTECTIVE TARIFF THAT WILL ENCOURAGE
DOMESTIC INDUSTRIES AND GIVE EMPLOYMENT
TO ALL OUR PEOPLE; ADVOCATING RECIPROCITY.

A DOCTRINE WHICH WILL OPEN AN UNLIMITED
MARKET FOR THE AMERICAN FARM AND THE
AMERICAN FACTORY A DOCTRINE BEQUEATHED
TO THIS GENERATION BY THE NOW SAINTED
JAMES G. BLAINE.

Upon these issues the Republican party comes confidentially to the people, asking for their suffrage, appealing not to their prejudice but to their reason, not to their passions, but to their judgment. In this holy crusade we are lead by that valiant champion of the people's rights, "that advance agent of prosperity," Maj. William McKinley. On the other hand we find the Bryanized democrats, populists, and believers in Coin's Financial School arrayed in a solid phalanx against these cherished principles which we so ardently believe in.

WILSON LAW CLOSED
FACTORIES.

The repeal of the McKinley law in 1893 closed down factories and manufactories by the hundred and deprived tens of thousands of American workmen of employment.

UNDER THE OPERATIONS OF THE MCKINLEY LAW THE WAGE EARNERS OF THE UNITED STATES WERE RECEIVING EVERY SATURDAY NIGHT A LITTLE OVER $41,000,000. UNDER THE OPERATION OF THE WILSON LAW THEY ARE RECEIVING A LITTLE LESS THAN $19,000,000 AS A SATURDAY NIGHT PAY ROLL, A FALLING OFF OF OVER $22,000,000 PER WEEK TO THE WAGE EARNERS OF THIS COUNTRY.

If you ask me what has been the most unfortunate and appalling result of this wonderfully shrunken pay roll, I will answer by saying that American workingmen by the thousands have lost the roof that covered their heads for themselves and families, have been turned into the highways and are beggars to-day in the most unfortunate sense of the word. The questions of free trade and protection however, have practically been relegated into the background this year, and the sixteen-headed monster of free silver pushed to the front.

FELLOW CITIZENS, FREE TRADE AND FREE SILVER ARE TWIN SISTERS OF INFAMY, THE ASSERTIONS OF MR. HARVEY TO THE CONTRARY NOTWITHSTANDING.

It was the province of the Republican party four years ago to send forth its protests and warnings against free trade, and to-day with equal vehemence it is sending forth its warnings against destroying the high standard of our nation's finance, and reducing this country to a second class basis of silver monometallism.

BREAD AND BUTTER
THE ISSUE.

FELLOW CITIZENS, THE PAPER ISSUE IN THIS CAMPAIGN IS ONE OF FINANCE, BUT THE REAL ISSUE IS ONE OF BREAD AND BUTTER. FREE TRADE DURING THE LAST THREE YEARS HAS PAUPERIZED ITS TENS OF THOUSANDS, BUT THIS FREE SILVER CRAZE, IF PLACED UPON OUR STATUTE BOOKS, WILL PAUPERIZE ITS HUNDREDS OF THOUSANDS.

My friends, I believe, and believe most earnestly, with every throb of my heart, that in the present campaign the Republican party is the only true friend silver has. We seek to elevate the silver dollar, our opponents seek to debase it. The Republican party has provided a redeemer for every silver dollar. Our opponents seek to destroy and alienate this redeemer. If the silver dollar was not exchangeable with gold, it would not be worth any more than a Mexican dollar, or not as much, for there is less silver in it. Coin's Financial School and free silver advocates generally, have much to say about the money of the constitution. Let me say to you, the money of the constitution was based upon the relative market value of the two metals. The history of the last 404 years, from 1492 to 1896, is replete with evidence proving beyond the question of a doubt that the relative or market value of these metals is continually changing. When Columbus discovered America in 1492, ten ounces of silver would purchase one ounce of gold; when the Pilgrim Fathers landed on the rocky and barren coast of New England in 1620, thirteen ounces of silver would purchase one ounce of gold; in 1792 fifteen ounces of silver would purchase one ounce of gold. In 1873 one ounce of gold would not purchase sixteen ounces of silver. To-day one ounce of gold will purchase almost thirty-two ounces of silver.

THIS FLUCTUATION OF VALUES OF THE TWO METALS IS CONTROLLED, NOT BY LAWS WE SPREAD UPON OUR STATUTE BOOKS, BUT BY THE LAW OF SUPPLY AND DEMAND, GOVERNED BY THE COST OF PRODUCTION.

JACKSON AND JEFFERSON.

The patriotism and statesmanship of Andrew Jackson and Thomas Jefferson were untainted in 1792 by the dangerous influence of a coterie of silver barons. They simply ascertained as nearly as they could the relative or market value of the two metals, and determined the legal from the commercial ratio, placed them side by side and started our mints going with the unlimited coinage of gold and silver at the ratio of 15 to 1. As a matter of fact they had overvalued silver; that is to say, the gold dollar was worth 100 cents, but the silver dollar was only worth 98 cents. Now the rank and file of our forefathers cared very little about the discrepancy of the 2 cents on the dollars, but the money changers were abroad in the land in 1792, the same as they are in 1896, and whenever a gold coin came into their possession it was quietly retired from circulation. In other words, the cheaper money drove out of circulation the higher priced money, and as a result, we had silver as the only hard money currency circulating in this country from 1792 to 1834. Let me quote Thomas Jefferson's own words. In speaking of the ratio of the two metals, he says:

"THE PROPORTION BETWEEN THE VALUES OF GOLD AND SILVER IS A MERCANTILE PROBLEM ALTOGETHER."

What statement could be clearer and more concise than that? It being a mercantile problem, it of course was understood to be subject to fluctuation and change. Accordingly, in 1834 our forefathers concluded as their first attempt at a double standard had utterly failed in keeping the two metals circulating side by side as money, that they would change the ratio from 15 to 1 to 16 to 1, which they did. It seems this ratio undervalued silver, that is to say, the gold dollar was still worth 100 cents, but the silver dollar was worth from 102 to 103 cents. Gold at once became the hard money circulating medium in this country, silver the higher priced money, was entirely retired by the money changers, bullion dealers and silversmiths. This is another illustration where the cheaper money drove out of circulation the higher priced money.

GREENBACKS WERE CHEAP MONEY.

In 1861 our country was engaged in civil war, and the greenbacks were issued as money, and were at once looked upon as a cheaper money than either gold or silver and immediately drove both gold and silver out of circulation and kept them out of circulation for seventeen years, or until we resumed specie payment in 1879. The history of these seventeen years is another instance where the cheaper money was victorious and drove out of circulation the higher priced money. Mr. Harvey no less than four times in his recent speech in this city gave the following definition of bimetallism: "Bimetallism is the right to use either of the two metals for money." This condensed answer bears about the same relation to the correct definition of bimetallism as the Boy Orator of the Platte compares with those intellectual giants whom he seeks to imitate, but without success, the immortal Washington and Lincoln. *(Applause)*. Bimetallism as is understood in the discussion of our financial question, is the use of both gold and silver as money; both legal tender money, and the legal ratio between the two metals determined from the commercial ratio. Throughout Mr. Harvey's published works and lectures we find him affirming the false principle that money is a creature of law, and that by operation of law the commercial ratio between gold and silver can be made to conform with the legal ratio of 16 to 1. Let us follow the author of "Coin's Financial School" for a few moments, and see where this false principle will carry us.

TO-DAY THE COMMERCIAL RATIO BETWEEN SILVER AND GOLD IS ABOUT 32 TO 1. MR. HARVEY CLAIMS THAT IF HIS THEORIES ARE SPREAD UPON OUR STATUTE BOOKS THAT IN A VERY SHORT TIME THE COMMERCIAL RATIO WILL BE 16 TO 1. IF MR. HARVEY POSSESSES THE SUPERHUMAN POWER OF REDUCING THE VALUE OF GOLD ONE-HALF, OR DOUBLING THE PRICE OF SILVER, WHICHEVER YOU WILL, AND BRING THEM TO A COMMERCIAL PARITY AT 16 TO 1, THEN INDEED WOULD HE BE FALSE TO THE CITIZENS OF THIS REPUBLIC IF HE DID NOT ADD A LITTLE MORE POWER TO HIS "KEELEY-MOTOR" THEORY, *(APPLAUSE)* AND MAKE THE COMMERCIAL RATIO BETWEEN GOLD AND SILVER 15 TO 1, THE SAME AS IT WAS IN 1792, OR BETTER STILL, IF IT IS A BLESSING TO HUMANITY TO LOWER THE RATIO BETWEEN GOLD AND SILVER, THEN APPLY A LITTLE MORE OF THIS OCCULT POWER AND MAKE THE RATIO 13 TO 1, THE SAME AS IT WAS IN 1620, WHEN OUR ANCESTORS CAME OVER IN THE

MAYFLOWER; OR APPLY THE SAME FORCE WITH
RENEWED ENERGY AND BRING THE RATIO DOWN
TO 10 TO 1, THE SAME AS IT WAS IN 1492. INDEED,
IF THIS PRINCIPLE IS A BOON TO HUMANITY,
AND HIS THEORIES ARE NOT FALSE, WHY NOT
PUSH THE WORK ALONG AND MAKE THE RATIO
BETWEEN GOLD AND SILVER 1 TO 1? *(APPLAUSE.)*

My fellow citizens, in following my friend Harvey, you are
led into a labyrinth abounding with impossibilities and as
impracticable as the theory of perpetual motion. When the earth
is proven to be flat instead of a globe, when water runs up-hill,
when the law of gravitation ceases to be operative, when the tail
wags the dog and not the dog the tail, then, and not till then, may
we seriously consider these perpetual motion, "Keeley Motor"
theories of Mr. Harvey and other double standard advocates.
(Great Applause). If we were unable to keep both metals circulating
side by side when there was a slight discrepancy of only two or
three cents in their intrinsic value, does any intelligent or sane
man believe for a moment whether he is a student of Coin's
Financial School or not, that if we throw open our mints to the
free and unlimited coinage of 52-cent dollars, that they would
not at once drive out of circulation the $630,000000 of gold, now
constituting more than one-third of our circulating medium?
If gold, so important a factor in our medium of exchange both
at home and abroad, should retire before silver—the cheaper
money (and the light of experience surely proves that it would)
can any one doubt that we would at once go on to a silver basis?
Can any one doubt that the $625,300,000 of silver now used as
money in this country would not instantly be cut in two so far
as its purchasing power is concerned—that is, shrink from 100
cents, its face or nominal value, to 52 cents, its bullion value? In
the light of past experience it would surely be a sad commentary
on our intelligence as an enlightened nation, if we had learned
nothing in 100 years. If the illustrious Hamilton and Jefferson

were alive, they would, by pursuing the same policy which actuated them in determining the money of the constitution, fix the ratio to-day at about 32 to 1, simply because the relative or market value of the two metals has varied to that extent.

HONESTY AND SOBER
JUDGMENT NEEDED.

My countrymen, the questions involved in the present campaign merit and deserve your most careful thought and study. It is the sober, honest judgment of the thinking, reading, investigating American citizen that the Republican party is relying upon for its support. Let me give you a few facts which possibly you will consider worthy of remembrance:

FIRST. EVERY FREE AND UNLIMITED COINAGE COUNTRY IN THE WORLD IS ON A SILVER BASIS.

SECOND. THERE IS NOT A GOLD STANDARD COUNTRY ON EARTH BUT WHAT USES BOTH GOLD AND SILVER AS MONEY.

THIRD. THERE IS NOT A SILVER STANDARD COUNTRY IN THE WORLD THAT USES ANY GOLD WHATEVER AS MONEY; AND

LASTLY, THERE IS NOT A SILVER STANDARD COUNTRY TO BE FOUND IN THE GREAT OCEAN OF COMMERCE THAT ROLLS ALL 'ROUND THE WORLD THAT HAS ONE-FOURTH AS MUCH MONEY PER CAPITA AS HAS THE UNITED STATES AND OTHER GOLD STANDARD COUNTRIES.

China, Japan, India, Mexico and most of the South American states are on a silver basis. The United States, England, France, Germany, Belgium, Sweden and others are on a gold basis.

One of the most interesting facts which the student of finance will encounter, is the vast difference of the amount of money per capita between the gold standard and the silver standard countries.

PER CAPITA OF MONEY.

In the countries on a silver basis we find the Central American states with a per capita of $3.78, Japan with a per capita of only $4.09, India $3.33, China $2.08, Mexico $5.47. Now note the difference between these countries and a few that I will mention that are on a gold basis:

The United States has a per capita of $21.10, England $19.98, France $36.70, Germany $18.78, Belgium $27.82.

In this connection, fellow citizens, let me impress upon your minds the facts that you cannot go into any country on the face of the earth where its mints are open to free and unlimited coinage of silver and find a single gold coin circulating among the people, moreover, that the silver standard country does not exist where the United States gold dollar, the United States silver dollar, or the United States paper dollar will not purchase twice as much merchandise as any dollar which you can find circulating among its people. I challenge the author of Coin's Financial School or the Demosthenes of Nebraska, William Jennings Bryan, or any one else, to successfully contradict this statement.

I AM A BIMETALLIST.

Personally, I am a bimetallist, and confidentially believe the republican party, guided by its wisdom and patriotism, will during the McKinley administration, devise ways and means by international agreement of autimatically adjusting the unsolved problem of true bimetallism, and keep both gold and silver on a parity at some given ratio. Silver will then be lifted from its place as one of the commodities of the earth and dignified as money, side by side with gold. To-day, I am a bimetallist, an ardent and devoted one, in the sense that I desire to see both gold and silver circulating side by side as money, and in the sense that we can have a greater per capita of money in this country by using both gold and silver as currency, than we possibly could by driving gold out of circulation, but fellow citizens, I disbelieve utterly in the possibility of a double standard. The phrase, "double standard" is a contradiction of terms. Standard means "correct measure," and you cannot have two different correct measures of value any more than you can have two different correct yard sticks, or two different correct results from a mathematical problem, or two different correct cyclometers on a bicycle. It one is right the other is wrong, and that is all there is to it. England tried the imaginary double standard for 470 years, and never succeeded in keeping the two metals circulating side by side, and finally gave it up as an utter failure. France with all the ingenuity of her inventive people, changed the ratio of gold and silver 118 times in twelve years in trying to balance on the double standard tight rope. We commenced trying it in 1792, and went on to a silver basis and remained there for 42 years, or until we changed the ratio from 15 to 1, to 16 to 1, in 1834. This change of ratio placed us on a gold basis, where we remained for a number of years. In 1861 we went on a paper basis and remained there for a number of years, and finally went back on to a gold basis in the common accepted understanding of the question, where we have since remained and the progress and prosperity of the United States during the last third of a century has been without a precedent in the history of the civilized world, and yet, I believe with my whole heart, that in the evolution of this financial question, hastened on by agitation, a plain of understanding will be reached higher and beyond that which has ever heretofore obtained in any of the civilized nations of the earth, and it will come through deliberations and councils in the republican party—the party of progress—and when it comes it will lighten the burdens and bless humanity.

THE CRIME OF '73.

Mr. Harvey and all silver advocates talk to us about the crime of 1873. Let me say here and now there was no crime committed in 1873, directly or indirectly.

IF THERE WAS A CRIME COMMITTED, SENATORS JONES AND STEWART OF NEVADA, THE PRESENT HIGH PRIESTS IN THE SILVER MOVEMENT WERE THE CHIEF CONSPIRATORS, FOR THEN, AS NOW, THEY WERE AMONG THE LARGEST SILVER MINE OWNERS IN THE UNITED STATES, AND THEY VOTED FOR THE BILL.

Prior to 1873 we had coined in this country, all told, about 8,000000 of silver dollars, since 1873 we have coined up to January 1st, 1896, $547 914,340 of silver, about $426,000,000 of which are standard dollars. Since January 1st, 1896, we have coined over $13,000,000 of standard dollars. During last August we coined 2,650,000 of silver dollars, and the profit to the government—the people—was between $800,000 and $900,000.

WEBSTER SAYS: "DEMONETIZATION IS TO DEPRIVE OF VALUE, OR TO WITHDRAW FROM USE AS CURRENCY."

Does it look very much as though we had withdrawn silver from use as currency? In what way have we deprived silver of value? It is a full legal tender for all debts, public and private, and without limit as to amount, and has been for the last eighteen years. These, fellow citizens, are facts which you will not find within the covers of "Coin" Harvey's books, it looks as though we had added value to it, since the silver dollar circulates side by side with the gold dollar, notwithstanding its bullion value is 48 cents less than its nominal or face value.

CONSISTENT FRIEND OF SILVER.

THE REPUBLICAN PARTY HAS EVER BEEN THE CONSISTENT FRIEND OF SILVER AND TO-DAY IS IRREVOCABLY COMMITTED TO THE DOCTRINE OF INTERNATIONAL BIMETALLISM, BUT IS UNALTERABLY OPPOSED TO SILVER MONOMETALLISM.

For one, I am not willing to see all the gold in this country driven out of circulation and the purchasing power of silver reduced to its bullion value. In other words, I am not ready to see the per capita of money in this country reduced fully one-half and our nation doing business on a Mexicanized silver basis. Wages are the last schedule to advance, and as fully 95 per cent, of the male adults in the United States are wage, salary or fee earners, there would be almost universal want, misery and suffering bequeathed to these people, because of such a reckless, unpatriotic and unbusiness-like experiment. What party then is the real friend of silver? The party that is trying to maintain the parity of the two metals, or the party that is protesting friendship in unstinted terms and yet committed to the folly of reducing silver to its bullion value? Fellow citizens the proposition in a nutshell is this:

THE REPUBLICAN PARTY BELIEVES THAT THE
COINAGE OF SILVER SHOULD BE RESTRICTED BY
LAW AND COINED ON GOVERNMENT ACCOUNT.
MR. BYRAN AND HIS FOLLOWERS BELIEVE IN THE
FREE AND UNLIMITED COINAGE OF SILVER ON
PRIVATE ACCOUNT. WHEN THE GOVERNMENT
COINS SILVER, UNDER EXISTING LAWS, IT GETS
THE DIFFERENCE BETWEEN THE COST OF THE
BULLION AND THE STAMP THAT IS PLACED UPON
IT. THIS IS KNOWN AS THE GAIN OR SEIGNIORAGE
AND IS PAID INTO THE TREASURY OF THE
UNITED STATES THE SAME AS IS PROVIDED BY
LAW REGULATING SUBSIDIARY COINS. IN THIS
WAY EVERY MECHANIC, EVERY FARMER, EVERY
LABORER, IN FACT EVERY CITIZEN OF THE
UNITED STATES GETS HIS PROPORTIONATE SHARE
OF THIS GAIN.

DO NOT
DEMAND BIMETALLISM.

What "Coin" Harvey and the advocates of free silver demand
is not bimetallism, but the unlimited coinage of the silver dollar,
not at the just ratio of 32 to 1, but at the unjust ratio of 16 to
1, not on government account, but on private account. To-day
the government—the people—are receiving the benefit of the
48 cents on each silver dollar coined, that being the difference
between the cost of the bullion and the face value of the dollar.
The government—the people-will lose these 48 cents if silver is
coined on private account. The question is, my countrymen, who
will get these 48 cents on each dollar, who will be benefitted by
this change? We know the government will lose 48 cents on each
dollar, the question is, who will receive it, or will this profit, now
accruing to the government—the people—be lost as completely

as the value of this building would be to the owner if it burned to ashes and there was no insurance? *(Applause.)* I am pretty well acquainted with the mining business, have spent many years of my life in the mining districts of the west, and am the owner to-day of mining properties in Oregon and in Colorado, and also largely interested in one of the most noted silver mining properties in Old Mexico, and I know whereof I speak, when I say to you that English capitalists and American silver kings own a majority of the stock of nearly every incorporated silver mining company in this country of any prominence.

It is beginning to look to me like "there was a pretty good-sized African in the wood pile somewhere." (Laughter and applause.)

FREE TRADE SHOULD
BE UNDONE.

Eight years ago, and again four years ago, through the influence of the Cobden Club, England attempted to subdue America. She succeeded in prostrating our industries, impoverishing our people, and increasing our public debt, but let us hope that the intelligence of American citizens will rise up in its full might and undo the free trade blunder of 1892. It now looks to me as if there was a gigantic trust of silver kings and English capitalists attempting to again subdue free America. Evidently there never was such a concert of action in the United States as has taken place during the last few months in regard to this silver question. The rapidity with which it has travelled all over this country, to say the least, has been phenomenal. There is an old saying, that "a falsehood will travel a thousand miles while truth is getting its boots on." Fellow citizens, go forth and tell the misguided advocates of free silver and believers in the false theories of "Coin's" Financial School to rejoice in their strength while it is called to-day, for, by the living God "truth has its boots on" and is marching triumphantly out among the people, tearing away the webs and veils of delusion and hypocrisy and appealing to the people, not to their passions, but to their intelligence, their reason and their honor. The people are not ready to advance by going backwards, they are not ready to be Chinaized, to be Japanized, South Americanized, Mexicanized or subsidized by a coterie of silver barons and English capitalists, who are attempting by stealth to nail the wage earners and farmers of this country to an unholy cross of depreciated silver. *(Applause.)*

GOES AFTER BRYAN.

William Jennings Bryan tells us in his Knoxville, Tennessee, speech, that there is no danger of a silver flood. "Coin" Harvey makes the same statement, notwithstanding the world's production of silver for the year 1894, at only about 63 cents an ounce, amounted to the fabulous sum of $216,000,000, a greater annual production than ever before in the history of the world, and only exceeded by the output of silver for the year of 1805, which amounted to $235,000,000, and still he claims there is no danger of a silver flood. All that Mr. Bryan asks for is, that the reins of government and the keys of the United States treasury be turned over to himself and his followers, and they will try the experiment. I hardly think the people of the United States are ready to invest in any more political experiments. The experiment of four years ago has proved quite enough. No flood of silver! The effrontery and insult to the intelligence of mankind by this degenerate democracy and silver advocates surpasses understanding. *(Applause.)* Fellow citizens, the so-called crime of 1873 is a myth and destitute of substance. The so-called conspiracy of that year is also a myth and without substance. You might just as well go out and from the housetop proclaim that the horse has been dehorserized, because of a huge conspiracy entered into by electricity and the bicycle. Why not ask that the

24

noble animal be rehorserized, so that its selling price will be $150 or $200, the same as it was in "ye olden times." *(Applause.)*

IMPROVED HARVESTING METHODS.

The old-fashioned methods of reaping the yellow fields of wheat has also been ousted by the conspiracy of the late improved harvester and binder. The old fashioned cradle has been decradleized. Why not form an alliance all over this country to recradleize the cradle, and make common warfare against the up-to-date binder? Even the old McCormick reaper has been dereaperized and the succeeding invention, the header, has been deheaderized, and who shall not say in this onward march of progress, in this wonderful advancement of our civilization, in this age of discovery and invention, that sooner or later the up-to-date binder of to day will not be debinderized by the inventive genius of some American citizen? *(Applause.)* Now, let us see, fellow citizens, what the so-called crime of 1873 has done for prices of various commodities. One of the stock declarations of Mr. Bryan and Mr. Harvey and their cohorts is that prices should be restored and wages should be increased. One of two things is very apparent, either the framers of the Chicago platform did not consult the statistics of the United States, or else they imagined the voters would not. "Coin" Harvey and the silver advocates generally seek to establish their position by quoting statistics of average prices of certain great commodities like wheat and cotton claiming that prices commenced falling in 1873, and their decline has continued ever since. These arguments are those of the delusionists and must crumble before the evidence and the facts. Let me say to you that prices did not commence falling in 1873, but in 1864-5.

WHY ARE THEY NOT HONEST?

If these men are not demagogues, pure and simple, why do they not inform the "dear people" why prices fell more during the eight years precedent 1873 than they have ever fallen since?

"COIN" HARVEY HAS NEVER EXPLAINED WHY, AND IF HE DID, HIS THEORY WOULD VANISH LIKE THE MIST BEFORE THE RISING SUN OF TRUTH.

For example, cotton fell from $1.01 1/2 in 1864, to 17 cents a pound in 1871. Or wheat for instance. The average farm price of wheat in the United States for the year 1874 was 94 cents a bushel, paper currency, or only 84 cents a bushel in gold. The average farm price of wheat in the United States for 1891 was 83 cents a bushel, the same in 1890, while in 1888 the average farm price of wheat in this country was 92 cents a bushel, or 6 cents a bushel higher than it was in 1874. Thus it will be seen that an unfair and false impression is trying to be created among the people by both Mr. Bryan and his followers. Perhaps Mr. Bryan and the free silver advocates would like to know where I get my statistics. I answer them by saying they are taken direct from the United States Statistical Abstract, which deservedly ranks high as an authority. In looking over this work I could not help wondering if "Coin" Harvey and our opponents who are shouting so loud and lustily for the free and unlimited coinage of silver and a restoration of prices, would not like to apply their cure-all to refined sugar, which was selling in 1872 at 12 3/5 cents per pound, and only 4 3/5 cents per pound in 1892, or for instance, illuminating oil was quoted in 1872 at 23 cents a gallon, and only 5 9/10 cents per gallon in 1892. Manufacturers of bar iron in 1872 were receiving $97.63 per ton for their product, and only $29.96 a ton in 1894. A keg of nails cost $5.46 in 1872, and $1.08 in 1894. A box of window glass that cost $3.40 in 1873, sold only at $1.70 in 1891. A carpet that cost $1.14 a yard in

1873, can be purchased today for 36 cents a yard. The steamboat transportation companies hauling wheat from Chicago to New York City, by lake and canal, are receiving a compensation to-day of a little less than 4 1/2 cents a bushel, but in 1873 they were receiving 24 1/2 cents per bushel, for every bushel they carried.

SHALL PRICES BE RESTORED.

The question is, do the people of the United States want these prices restored?

WE ARE WILLING AS AMERICANS THAT AMERICAN INDUSTRIES AND HOME COMPETITION SHALL ADJUST PRICES, BUT WE ARE NOT WILLING THAT PRICES OF LABOR SHALL BE ADJUSTED IN THIS COUNTRY BY AMERICAN WORKMEN ENTERING INTO COMPETITION WITH THE PAUPERIZED LABORERS OF EUROPE.

From the same reliable statistics and undoubted authority we find that wages have materially advanced in this country during the last third of a century. The increase from the old double standard wages of 1860 to those of 1890, have been no less than 58 per cent, in money, and 72 per cent, in purchasing power. This does not look very much like a falling off. I will admit that the price of wheat has declined and declined rapidly since 1892, but you must remember that Grover Cleveland was elected president that year and is still in the White House. Give us back a protection that protects, and we will not only insure abundance of labor for all our people, but will guarantee that farm products generally will command better prices. *(Applause).*

FELLOW CITIZENS, I EARNESTLY BELIEVE THAT "COIN" HARVEY AND ALL THOSE WHO ARE

ADVOCATING THE FREE AND UNLIMITED
COINAGE OF SILVER AT THE UNJUST AND UNTRUE
RATIO OF 16 TO 1, AS A NOSTRUM FOR OUR ILLS,
ARE ADVOCATING A THEORY AS MISLEADING AS
IT IS WICKED AND UNHOLY. NO THEORY MORE
FALSE WAS EVER ADVANCED OR CALCULATED
TO MORE THOROUGHLY DECEIVE THE EARNEST,
INDUSTRIOUS, GOD FEARING PEOPLE OF THIS
NATION.

Let us undo the free trade blunder of 1892 and we will hear no more about the mythical crime of 1873. *(Applause.)*

PROTECTIVE TARIFF THE REMEDY.

My friends, a tariff that protects; reciprocity that opens up a market for our surplus articles from the American farm and the American factory; a sound currency, and the business confidence which will follow, are the remedies for the unfortunate condition of bankruptcy into which the country has been submerged by political stupidity.

THE QUESTION IS SIMPLY ONE OF HONESTY OR DISHONESTY.

Shall thrift and economy be rewarded by robbery? Shall the widow's mite and the savings deposited in the banks of this country be cut in two by changing our money to silver monometallism? Shall the two and a half billions of school bonds from all over the country, held by English and American capitalists and payable in gold, be doubled, and a double tax fall upon the shoulders of the tax payers of this nation? Shall the toilers of this land, the wage-earners on farm and in factory, be robbed every Saturday night of one-half of their weekly wages?

LABORERS SHALL BE
HONESTLY REWARDED.

NO. THIS BLOT OF REPUDIATION SHALL NOT SMIRCH THE UNTARNISHED ESCUTCHEON OF AMERICAN PATRIOTISM, NEITHER SHALL THE TOILING MASSES RECEIVE AS THEIR REWARD FOR HONEST LABOR A "MESS OF DEPRECIATED SILVER POTTAGE."

We are now asked to desert the old ship of state that has carried this nation through many storms, through many conflicts, and invariably anchored us in the snug harbor of safety and maintained our country on the map of the world, and added many stars to the old flag. We are asked by these new and false prophets of finance to destroy this grand old ship, freighted with the hopes and ambitions of seventy millions of free American citizens; this old ship tested by time, tried by adversity, taut and trim as a May queen and invincible as a Bessemer steel iron cladder, a ship that was launched by Washington and the patriots of 100 years ago, and piloted by such noble men as Lincoln, Grant, Garfield and Hayes. We are asked to desert this ship of known safety, and embark in an untried craft and sail away on the turged waters of an unknown sea. A craft manned by a free silver captain, piloted by free tradeism, and ballasted with bombs of anarchy and repudiation; a craft whose very slimy plank is reeking with condemnation; whose mutinous crew are ready to scuttle her in mid ocean; whose worthless and shoddy sails are fanned by the angry breath of high heaven; and whose nearest port is bankruptcy and perdition. (Long continued applause.)

MY FELLOW CITIZENS, THE TRUE SOLUTION OF
THE PRESENT FINANCIAL DEPRESSION LIES ALONG
OTHER LINES, AND THIS BRINGS US FACE TO FACE
WITH THE REAL PROBLEM.

Perhaps you have noticed already in this campaign that
no one is quite so disgusted with remarks on the tariff as a
Byranized democrat or a populist? The impoverished condition
of the country, resulting from the free trade crime of 1893 is so
apparent on every hand that when we lay the skeletons at their
doors they frankly confess judgment, but tell us that other
questions of more vital importance are now before the people.

MY FRIENDS, THE ENDLESS CHAIN OF AMERICAN
PROSPERITY HAS BEEN BROKEN AND NEVER WILL
BE MENDED UNTIL THE DRAWN FIRES FROM
OUR FURNACES ARE REKINDLED AND THE FREE
TRADE SMOKE CONSUMERS ARE REMOVED FROM
THE TALL CHIMNEYS IN OUR MANUFACTURING
DISTRICTS. *(APPLAUSE.)*

A PRINCIPLE UPHELD BY STATESMEN.

It is not in any exulting spirit that we refer to a protective
tariff, but rather because it is a great and underlying principle
of national prosperity; a principle bequeated to this nation by
Washington, upheld by Henry Clay, fostered by Abraham
Lincoln, championed by William McKinley, and supported by
the reciprocity of James J. Blaine. Prior to the free trade crime of
1892, we heard nothing about a diminished gold reserve.

IN THOSE HALCYON DAYS CONFIDENCE FLEW
ABROAD IN THE LAND ON THE WINGS OF
PROSPERITY.

Capital was freely invested and labor employed at the highest wages. The gold reserve occasioned no uneasiness and required no thought. Instead of acting as an alarmist it steadily grew, acting as a balance wheel to an ever-increasing confidence. The surplus was employed in paying off the national debt; and during President Harrison's administration our national indebtedness was reduced almost as much as it has been increased by the present administration. What has happened during the last three and a half years of grace?

THE ALLURING AND MUSICAL HUM OF INDUSTRY
IS NO LONGER HEARD IN THE LAND OF FREEDOM.
THE PENDULUM OF TIME HAS SWUNG BACK
AND REVEALED TO THE AMERICAN PEOPLE THE
GHASTLY SKELETON OF WANT AND FORCED
IDLENESS CONCEALED IN THE FREE TRADE
CLOSET.

Our great commercial institutions have fallen into a most deplorable and unhappy state, misery and want, with pinched and sorrowful countenances are walking hand in hand up and down by deserted workshops. The honest face of toil blushes as hunger drives him to eat the bread of charity. The stilled wheels of industry throughout our land, and deserted and idle farms are indeed eloquent in their silence in behalf of a protective tariff. *(Applause.)* Capital that was formerly employed in manufacturing enterprises has been withdrawn, while the balance of trade with other nations is frightfully against us.

ENGLAND HAS BEEN SERVED.

IF ENGLAND HAD HAD A POLITICAL PARTY
MANUFACTURED TO ORDER BY THE MOST

31

SKILLED ARTISANS OF THE EARTH, SHE COULD
NOT HAVE HAD ONE MADE THAT WOULD MORE
FAITHFULLY SERVE HER COMMERCIAL PURPOSES
THAN HAS THE PRESENT ADMINISTRATION.

Let us briefly inquire into the cause. Take, for instance, the
sheep and wool industry, which a few years ago was a prominent
one in your state. Under the stimulus of protection, we had in
this country in 1884, 50,500,000 sheep. Then Grover Cleveland
was elected president, and this was followed by the democratic
free wool indictment of 1885, known as the Mills bill. The
wool growers of America became alarmed, they fattened and
sold their sheep to the butchers by the millions. This slaughter
continued for four years, or until Gen. Harrison was elected
to the presidency in 1888. The authentic statement shows that
the number of sheep had been reduced in this country from
50,500,000 in 1884 to 41,300,000 in 1888. President Harrison's
election stopped the slaughter, and under the stimulus of the
McKinley law the industry gained rapidly and at the close of
Mr. Harrison's administration the total number of sheep in the
United States was 47,800,000. *(Applause.)* In 1892 Mr. Cleveland
was again elected president. This was followed by the repeal of
the McKinley law and the enactment of legislation hostile to the
wool industry. During the last three and a half years the number
of sheep in this country has been reduced from 47,800,000 to
38,500,000, or fewer sheep than there was in this country in
1873, or at any time since the so-called crime of that year. So
much fellow citizens, for the democratic free wool joke on the
American people.

HE TALKS OF WOOL.

Now let us talk for a few moments about the price of wool. For
ten years preceding the repeal of the McKinley law, the average

price of Ohio X.X.Washed wool in the Boston market was a little over 31 1/5 cents per pound. April 1, 1896 wool was quoted in the same market at 18 cents a pound. Such a startling contrast in prices needs no comments. As millions of our sheep were slaughtered we were compelled to import wool and woolen textiles into this country sending our money abroad, which should have been paid to the American farmer and sheep raiser. Instead of this we paid our money over to foreigners in exchange for wool and woolen textiles, which came into this country like a flood when the McKinley law was repealed and the duty removed. The result was that the woolen mills of America were practically all shut down and thousands upon thousands of American workingmen and women were thrown out of employment, and in turn, were unable to purchase the products from the American farm. No wonder the American farmer found a ready market for his potatoes in 1892, when all our people were employed, at from 50c to 60c a bushel; and to-day, when our people are unemployed, the farm price of potatoes is from 25c to 30c a bushel. Let us see what sort of a stewardship has been going on in this country for the last few years. For the twenty-five months ending November 1, 1892, our balance of trade with other nations was in our favor to the extent of $28,245,641. That is what the McKinley law and protection did for this country. That, fellow citizens, is what we call good business methods. Selling to other nations more than we purchased from them to the extent of $28,245,641, or an average of $1,129,822 per month, or $37,660 per day. *(Applause.)*

WHAT THE RECORD IS.

Now, let us look at Mr. Cleveland's record for the fifteen months ending December 1, 1895—this, you will remember, was under the Wilson bill. We find the balance of trade, instead of being in our favor, was against us to the enormous amount of $70,494,044, or an average of $4,699,603 per month, or $153,653 per day. That, fellow citizens, is a pretty good sized daily loss. That is what we call remarkably poor business methods, and so does every one within the hearing of my voice who is disposed to be fair in the consideration of this question. But why speak further of the evils of free trade, or multiply examples of the blessings of protection. The record of the last three and a half years has been an object lesson, both impressive and eloquent. It is gratifying to note that some of the ultra free traders in 1892 are the most pronounced protectionists in 1896. Many of the old time democrats who are proud of the traditions of their party, proud of the principles which they have cherished for so many years, are refusing to follow the platform adopted by the degenerate democracy of 1896. Let us mete out justice to whom justice is due.

WHEN THE FLAG OF OUR COUNTRY, WAVING ABOVE FORT SUMTER WAS FIRED UPON BY THE ENEMIES OF GOOD GOVERNMENT, THOUSANDS UPON THOUSANDS OF THE DEMOCRATS OF THE NORTH FORGOT THEIR POLITICS, SHOULDERED THEIR MUSKETS AND BECAME PATRIOTS. (APPLAUSE.) THIS YEAR OF GRACE, 1896, WHEN THE GUNS OF ANARCHY AND SOCIALISM ARE DIRECTED AGAINST THE SUPREME COURT OF THE UNITED STATES AND THE NATION'S HONOR AND CREDIT, THESE SAME DEMOCRATS BY THE TENS OF THOUSANDS ARE TURNING FROM THAT PLATFORM OF REPUDIATION AND ARE THE STANCHEST OF PATRIOTS. (APPLAUSE.)

SPIRIT OF REVOLUTION.

It cannot be denied that a spirit of wantonness and revolution prevailed at the Chicago convention, repudiation was openly advocated on the floor of the convention hall and made a part of the platform adopted. The red hand of anarchy grappled the throats of all who dared oppose the extreme measures advocated by that seething sea of restless agitators. I wish to draw a line of demarkation, clear and distinct, between the old Simon-pure democracy of Hamilton and Jefferson, and this new degenerate democracy of Bryan, Tillman and Altgeld. It is true the framers of the Chicago platform claim the name, but the tenants and faith are strangely at variance with the traditions and principles of the old Jeffersonian doctrine. My countrymen, it is not alone the volume of money which the people want, but they demand its activity in trade and commerce. If you ask me how this can best be accomplished, I will answer by saying, protect American industries and universal confidence will surely follow. *(Applause.)*

REAT IS CONFIDENCE.

CONFIDENCE IS THE SHIBBOLETH OF PROSPERITY.

CONFIDENCE THAT GOOD DOLLARS MEAN WELL PAID LABOR.

CONFIDENCE THAT WELL PAID LABOR MEANS GOOD TIMES.

CONFIDENCE THAT WAGES PAID TO AMERICAN WORKINGMEN WILL POSSESS THE SAME PURCHASING POWER AS THE BEST MONEY IN THE CIVILIZED WORLD.

CONFIDENCE THAT A PENSION POLICY, JUST AND GENEROUS TO OUR LIVING HEROES, WILL BE RESTORED.

CONFIDENCE THAT NO OLD SOLDIER IS TO BE
DEPRIVED OF HIS QUARTERLY CHECK WITHOUT
TRIAL BY JUDGE OR JURY.

CONFIDENCE THAT THE REPUBLICAN PARTY
WILL MAINTAIN A REDEEMER FOR EVERY SILVER
DOLLAR COINED.

CONFIDENCE THAT A RETURN OF THE
REPUBLICAN PARTY TO POWER WILL START
EVERY MILL AND FACTORY IN THIS COUNTRY,
WITHOUT THE AID OR CONSENT OF ANY OTHER
NATION OR NATIONS ON THE FACE OF THE
EARTH.

CONFIDENCE THAT INTERNATIONAL
BIMETALLISM, SO ABLY ADVOCATED DURING
PRESIDENT HARRISON'S ADMINISTRATION, WILL
BE VIGOROUSLY PROMOTED BY THE MC'KINLEY
ADMINISTRATION. (GREAT APPLAUSE.)

CONFIDENCE THAT A VOTE FOR MC'KINLEY AND
HOBERT IS A VOTE FOR THE HOME AND THE
FIRESIDE.

CONFIDENCE THAT VERMONT AND MAINE HAVE
PENCILED A BRIGHT PROPHECY OF HOPE IN THE
EASTERN SKY.

CONFIDENCE THAT THE DRAGON HEAD MONSTER
OF STATE RIGHTS IS NOT TO BE RESURRECTED IN
THIS COUNTRY. *(APPLAUSE.)*

CONFIDENCE THAT SOUND MONEY AND
PROTECTION ARE THE PILLARS OF JACKIN AND

BOAZ IN THE TEMPLE OF AMERICAN HONOR AND PROSPERITY.

CONFIDENCE THAT THE SUPREME COURT OF THE UNITED STATES IS TO REMAIN OUR BULWARK OF JUSTICE AND ALL THE GATES OF HELL SHALL NOT PREVAIL AGAINST IT. *(APPLAUSE.)*

PROUD OF BEING
A REPUBLICAN.

Fellow citizens, I am a Republican and proud of my party's history. The history of the United States has been made rich and resplendent with victories and achievements of our party. We are proud of our nation's history from its earliest dawn down to the present, and for the valuable lessons it has taught. We would not expunge or obliterate a single line. We accept it as a whole, from Plymouth Rock to Bunker Hill, from Bunker Hill to Fort Sumter, from Fort Sumter to Appomattox, and from Appomattox down to the campaign of 1896. We dedicate crowns of laurel for the giants who have evolved the mighty principles and tenets of the republican party—Washington and Grant, Blaine and Logan, Sherman and Garfield, Harrison and McKinley, and most of all, that gentle soul, that man of equal poise, whose peer has never lived since the days of blessed Galilean—Abraham Lincoln! *(Applause.)* Our history is one of greatness and sublimity. Its pages are rich with the names of orators more eloquent than a Burke, with the names of statesmen more acute than the "Iron Chancellor" and the names of warriors greater and mightier than Napoleon.

IN THE DARK AND TURBULENT DAYS OF THE REBELLION, THE REPUBLICAN PARTY, WITH THE ASSISTANCE OF DEMOCRATIC PATRIOTS, SAVED

THIS NATION, WHILE NOW IN THE CLOSING DAYS
OF THE NINETEENTH CENTURY, BY THE LIVING
GOD, PATRIOTS WILL SAVE AND PROTECT OUR
NATION'S HONOR.

Ours is the greatest nation on earth, and the possibilities of
the future are almost limitless; if we make no mistake in the great
principles of protection, reciprocity and a sound currency, which
have for their immediate object the betterment of the conditions
of the wage-earners of this land.

MARCHING TO
GREATEST VICTORY.

Following the leadership of our gallant standard bearer, that
brave civilian soldier on the field of battle, that statesman without
a peer, that friend of the toiling millions, that companion of every
old soldier, that invincible leader of men, Major McKinley, we are
advancing proudly on to the greatest political victory of modern
times. In the life of Major William McKinley, we find nothing
but purity and ability, bravery and compassion, and I promise
you that on the fourth day of next March he will be inaugurated
president of this republic; a republic whose flag, "Old Glory," the
stars and stripes, floats over seas and land, peerless and without
price, the emblem of power and protection to all. My friends, we
must restore our protective system. Already it has accomplished
wonders for the laborers of America, and its mission in behalf
of prosperity and posterity has only commenced. It has enabled
us to perfect a system of finance that is a marvel to all nations,
and has raised our credit to a place among the first countries
of the earth. It has elevated the manhood of every American
citizen, dignified labor, and instilled a more universal education
throughout our land than can be found in any other civilized
country on the face of the globe. It has made the flag of our

nation emblematical of love, liberty, protection, reciprocity, honor and all that is great and grand of human thought. Major William McKinley is our Bruce at Bannockburn in this struggle for national honor, unlimited labor and higher wages. In the golden casket of his great soul rests the immortal principles which we advocate, and in his heart burns the undying fire of love for America and American institutions. The righteousness of our cause is our strength, while he is our hope and will lead us triumphantly on to certain and splendid victory. *(Applause.)* But what about William Jennings Bryan?

> "Like a comet he rose to our vision,
> Like a comet he soon will depart;
> And 'tis certain his untimely going
> Will chill every popocrat's heart,
> In the coming cyclone of November
> We know his race will be run,
> And forever and aye, oh, let him remember,
> How our leader, McKinley has won."

(Great Applause.)